Severn Valley Railway Journey

David C. Williams

Silver Link Silk Editions

SLP

Severn Valley
Railway Journey

David C. Williams

Silver Link Publishing Ltd

The Severn Valley Railway
Kidderminster to Bridgnorth

This map shows the route of our 16-mile photographic journey over the Severn Valley Railway from Kidderminster to Bridgnorth. It is turned clockwise through slightly more than 90' to suit the format of this book, which allows more space to denote stations and structures. Our progress is from left to right across these two pages. Other railway routes in the immediate area, both open and closed, are also shown.

Section of line from Bewdley to Stourport and Hartlebury closed by BR in 1970 and lifted. Short stretch puchased by SVR Company in 1972

Cleobury Mortimer

The Wyre Forest line to Cleobury Mortimer, Tenbury Wells and Woofferton Junction closed by BR in 1962 and lifted.

Wyre Forest

NORTHWOOD HALT

ARLEY

Victoria Bridge

Wribbenhall Viaduct

River Severn

Burlish

Sandbourne Viaduct

BEWDLEY

Rifle Range Halt (Closed)

West Midlands Safari Park

Section of line between Milepost 144½ and Foley Park closed by BR north of Bewdley in 1969 and south of Bewdley in 1970. Purchased by the SVR Company. Passenger services to Bewdley from Bridgnorth restored in 1974 and onwards to Kidderminster during 1984.

Bewdley Tunnel

Stourport

Foley Park Halt (Closed)

Falling Sands Viaduct

KIDDERMINSTER TOWN (SVR)

Kidderminster (NR)

The Birmingham - Kidderminster - Worcester line is owned by Network Rail and is open for normal passenger and freight traffic

Hartlebury

to Worcester

to Birmingham

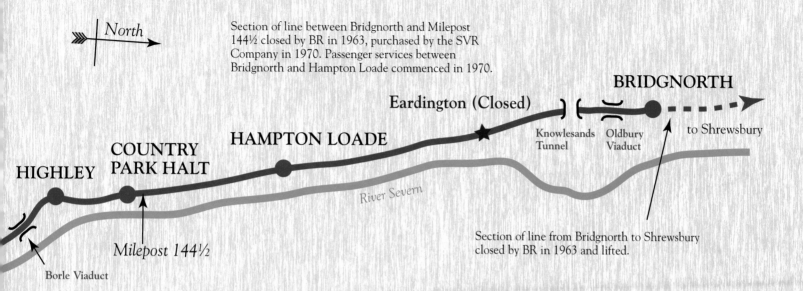

North

Section of line between Bridgnorth and Milepost 144½ closed by BR in 1963, purchased by the SVR Company in 1970. Passenger services between Bridgnorth and Hampton Loade commenced in 1970.

BRIDGNORTH

Eardington (Closed)

Knowlesands Tunnel

Oldbury Viaduct

to Shrewsbury

HAMPTON LOADE

HIGHLEY

COUNTRY PARK HALT

River Severn

Milepost 144½

Borle Viaduct

Section of line from Bridgnorth to Shrewsbury closed by BR in 1963 and lifted.

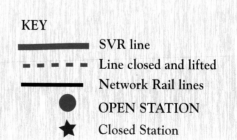

Distances

	Between stations	From Kidderminster
Kidderminster – Foley Park	1 mile 42 chains	
Foley Park – Bewdley	2 miles 5 chains	3 miles 47 chains
Bewdley – Northwood	1 miles 49 chains	5 miles 16 chains
Northwood – Arley	1 miles 77 chains	7 miles 13 chains
Arley – Highley	2 miles 27 chains	9 miles 40 chains
Highley – Country Park Halt	0 miles 75 chains	10 miles 35 chains
Country Park Halt – Hampton Loade	1 miles 17 chains	11 miles 52 chains
Hampton Loade – Eardington	2 miles 26 chains	13 miles 78 chains
Eardington – Bridgnorth	2 miles 14 chains	16 miles 12 chains

Note: there are 80 chains in one mile

KEY

———— SVR line

------ Line closed and lifted

———— Network Rail lines

● OPEN STATION

★ Closed Station

First published in 2014
British Library Cataloguing in
Publication Data

A catalogue record for this book is available from the British Library.

ISBN 978 1 85794 436 5

Silver Link Publishing Ltd
The Trundle
Ringstead Road
Great Addington
Kettering
Northants NN14 4BW

Tel/Fax: 01536 330588
email:
sales@nostalgiacollection.com
Website:
www.nostalgiacollection.com

Printed and bound in the
Czech Republic

Contents

Half title: A dramatic display of smoke and steam is produced by Great Western Railway Churchward/Collett 2-6-0 No 7325 as it rushes the 1 in 180 climb from Victoria Bridge to Arley station with a Kidderminster to Arley 'Santa Special' in December 1993. Soon, perfect peace will return to the Severn valley here. *Bob Green*

Title page: In a peaceful evening scene at Hampton Loade station on 14 September 2012, London & North Western Railway Webb-designed 'Coal Tank' No 1054 of 1888, running as LMSR No 7799, waits to leave for Bridgnorth. The departure time is 8.30pm for this photo charter train composed of three LMSR Stanier coaches. The engine finished in network service as BR No 58926 in 1958. *Alan Corfield*

Publisher's dedication

We raise our hats to Peter Victor Edkins, 1932-2013

The team at Silver Link Publishing would like to pay tribute to and remember Peter Edkins. Peter, a former headmaster, joined the SVR during the 1980s, first training as a Ticket Inspector, then a Guard. He was invited by the Guarantee Board of the SVR to form the Volunteer Liaison Office some 20 years ago, and 15 of those years were shared with Barry Moreton, who worked with Peter and said of him:

'How can I sum up my 15 years with him? I could comment upon his many achievements but the list is long so I will merely summarise that he was a very kind, loyal friend and would go to any lengths to help anyone. He always had time for people, especially where youngsters were concerned...'

We have published a number of books on the Severn Valley Railway over the past 25 years, and in that time we have been very fortunate to work and share time with many of the dedicated team of volunteers and staff that are the lifeblood of this fine railway. Our visits to Bewdley have been, and will be as far as possible in the future, timed to coincide with the days on which the Volunteer Liaison Office is open. Why? Because the warmth and friendship of the welcome that Peter Edkins nurtured so well 'as you popped your head round the door' will, we have no doubt, continue to enthuse and inspire us and the SVR volunteers of the future.

We raise our hats to you, Peter!

Introduction

Approaching its half-century as a heritage line, the Severn Valley Railway is a prolific supplier of steam trains. It operates on at least 240 days of the year, and on the busiest days requires up to six steam locomotives to satisfy the public demand, taking into account special trains as well as ordinary timetabled services.

In recent years, photographic technology has advanced immeasurably, and the creativity and expertise of railway photographers has more than kept pace with this. Also, computer images retain their quality during translation to the printed page, and moreover the good-quality colour prints of an earlier age lose little in conversion to the electronic form.

As editor of the quarterly *Severn Valley Railway News* magazine, your compiler is the happy recipient of some superb railway pictures for publication from both budding newcomers and seasoned experts. The limitations of the magazine format and schedule mean that many of the images are reproduced at a smaller than desirable size, or space precludes their inclusion completely.

This 'mini-coffee-table book' attempts to redress the balance a little, by presenting both previously seen and unseen images at worthwhile sizes. Arranged in northbound journey progression – i.e. 'down' from London in railway terms – here are presented a variety of locomotives and (mostly) appropriate trains in many different locations. The scenes are enlivened by widely differing weather conditions, and during all the four seasons.

The selection thus presented is the compiler's choice, so naturally he must take the blame for any lack of balance in the coverage. But it is a fact that some steam locomotives attract more photographic attention than others, and a compiler can only work with the best of what is sent. But all the pictures reproduced either (a) satisfy him personally or (b) are necessary to clarify the journey narrative.

I hope that you, the reader, share my enthusiasm for the scenes depicted, and that they form a happy reminder of a previous journey along the 'Valley', or maybe reinforce your determination to take your first ride in the near future!

BRIDGNORTH: Dennis Pike, a volunteer Travelling Ticket Inspector on the Severn Valley Railway enjoys his latest book purchase from the SVR's Bridgnorth shop in between duties. *Peter Townsend*

Kidderminster

My thanks are due to Linda Hartin of SVR Shops for suggesting the idea of this book, and to Peter Rowlands and Peter Townsend of Silver Link Publishing for their usual enthusiasm further along the book production process, always in my estimation an underrated activity. For proof checking, my thanks go to Tony Bending, David Mellor, John Smith, Mick York and all who made helpful observations.

Lastly, I must record my thanks to all the 'Severn Valley People', past, present and future, who made (and still make) all these scenes happen, whether by physical or mental effort, or financial support. After nearly 50 years of preservation, I still find it difficult to take in the wonderfully successful outcome of what we started then in such a humble way.

David C. Williams
February 2014

Left: Our journey starts at Kidderminster Town station, the southern terminus of today's Severn Valley Railway, in Comberton Hill. The red-brick station was built under preservation auspices and largely completed in 1984. It stands on the site of the one-time GWR Kidderminster goods yard. The building is a fairly accurate representation of Ross-on Wye station in Herefordshire, which was in passenger use from 1892 until 1964, and was later demolished. *John Stretton*

Right: Standing near the buffer stops at Kidderminster Town station on 2 August 2012 is Great Western Railway Collett-designed '8750' Class 0-6-0 pannier tank No 3650, which was built at Swindon in 1944. These 'panniers' were a common site in the Kidderminster area for more than 30 years. Normally based at Didcot in Oxfordshire, this particular loco was on loan to the SVR during the summer of 2012. *Steve Burdett*

Left: A scene redolent of British Railways Western Region in the 1950s presents itself at Kidderminster Town station on the sunny evening of 19 September 2008. The driver of the train is sitting ready for departure in the driving compartment of GWR-design Hawksworth auto-coach No W228W. His fireman, however, will no doubt be busy on the footplate of GWR Collett '4575' Class 2-6-2 tank No 5526, which is providing the power for this evening 'push and pull' departure to Bewdley. No 5526 was built at Swindon in 1928 and both the engine and coach are usually resident at Buckfastleigh, Devon. *Brian Harris*

Right: A wider view of the departure end of Kidderminster Town station shows the extensive goods shed, now the SVR carriage works, on the right, and the course of the Birmingham to Worcester line on the edge of the view. Southern Railway 'West Country' Class 4-6-2 No 34027 *Taw Valley*, here in the guise of No 34045 *Ottery St Mary*, awaits departure for Bridgnorth at 4.45pm on 5 April 2003. This locomotive was built at Brighton in 1946 to Bulleid's revolutionary design, and rebuilt in more conventional form at Eastleigh, Southampton, in 1957. Until 1983 the view from this spot embraced the busy sidings of Kidderminster goods yard. *Raymond Jones*

Train Staff

Clockwise from top left:
Fireman John Price and Driver
Dai Price. *Bob Sweet.*

Ticket Inspector *Roy* Millership.
Bob Warwick.

Buffet Car Stewards Julian and
June Williams. *Bob Warwick.*

Guard Brian Spaul.*Barry Moreton.*

Dining Car Steward Brian White.
Sharon Dredge.

Snack Trolley Attendant Stephen
Skewes. *Bob Warwick*

This is a view from the steps of the long footbridge (always called the 'wooden bridge') at Kidderminster Junction on 25 September 2009. The duty signalman in the SVR's Kidderminster box of 1988 oversees the departure of the 3.10pm Bridgnorth train headed by a matched pair of London Midland & Scottish Railway Ivatt-designed Class '2MT' engines. The leading engine, 2-6-2 tank No 41241, is usually to be found at Haworth, West Yorkshire, while 2-6-0 No 46443 is an SVR 'regular'. Both locomotives played a significant part in the reopening of their respective railways in the early preservation era. *Paul Dorney*

Kidderminster

Left: A gentle Kidderminster departure is being made by Bulleid 'Battle of Britain' Class 4-6-2 No 34070 *Manston*, in original 'air-smoothed' condition, at 9.25am on the bright morning of 25 September 2010. Ahead is the 'wooden bridge' and Network Rail's Kidderminster Junction signal box, built in 1957 and demolished in 2012. *Manston* was built at Brighton in 1949, it is usually to be found on the Swanage Railway in Dorset *Brian Harris*

Right: Here is the fireman's view from the footplate of GWR 'Manor' Class 4-6-0 No 7812 *Erlestoke Manor*, approaching Kidderminster with the 5.15pm train from Bridgnorth on 16 June 2003. Beyond the 'wooden bridge' can be glimpsed the carriage works, with the Network Rail line to Birmingham on the right. No 7812 is a Swindon product of 1939. *Raymond Jones*

Kidderminster

Left: A classic SVR scene is provided on the morning of 23 September 2011 by Caledonian Railway McIntosh '812' Class 0-6-0 No 828 pulling six of the SVR's unique set of LMSR coaches. The 9.50am train to Bridgnorth is passing under the impressive GWR-design signal gantry outside Kidderminster Town station. This '3F' Class locomotive, always based in Scotland, was on loan from its home at Aviemore in the Highlands for a period in 2011/12. Built at St Rollox works, Glasgow, in 1899, it was withdrawn as BR No 57566 at Ardrossan, Ayrshire, in 1963. *David Wilcock*

Above: The one-time Fort William turntable was installed at Kidderminster by SVR volunteers and completed in 1994. Here it is being used to turn GWR 'Manor' Class 4-6-0 No 7802 *Bradley Manor* during a photo session on 23 September 1995. *Jason Houlders*

Left: The carriage shed at Kidderminster was built in 2000 thanks largely to Heritage Lottery Fund support. Its four tracks hold 56 coaches. North Eastern Railway Worsdell-designed 'J72' Class 0-6-0 tank No 69023, actually built by BR at Darlington in 1951, is shunting BR Mark 1 stock in 'carmine and cream' livery on 23 September 2011. *David Wilcock*

Left: LNER Gresley-designed 'A4' Class 4-6-2 No 60009 *Union of South Africa*, built at Doncaster in 1937, accelerates out of Kidderminster with the 4.45pm Bridgnorth train on 10 August 2001. The set of former LMSR coaches behind the engine provides a reminder of Glasgow to Aberdeen trains of the mid-1960s. To the left is the carriage shed, with the Worcester line diverging on the right. *Raymond Jones*

Right: Viewed from Hoo Road bridge, Aggborough, Kidderminster, British Railways Standard 'Britannia' Class '7MT' 4-6-2 No 70013 *Oliver Cromwell* eases over recently renewed track with the 12.25pm train to Bridgnorth on 6 March 2009. The course of the Worcester line can just be discerned in the background. The engine, built at Crewe in 1952, is part of the National Railway Museum Collection at York. *Paul Dorney*

Left: In a scene reminiscent of an LNER publicity poster, Gresley 'A4' Class 4-6-2 No 4464 *Bittern* of 1937 heads an appropriate set of Gresley teak-bodied coaches forming the 8.50am Kidderminster to Bridgnorth train across Falling Sands Viaduct, Kidderminster, on 24 March 2012. The seven-arch, 132-yard-long viaduct spans firstly the River Stour and then (here)

Brindley's Staffordshire & Worcestershire Canal. *Alan Corfield*

Below: The only really urban landscape on the heritage Severn Valley Railway is at Foley Park, where there is a trading estate alongside the line, seen here on the left. The silos of the BSC sugar factory are visible through the trees top right; they were

demolished in 2012. Climbing towards the summit near the Stourport Road bridge on 17 January 2010 is LMR Ivatt Class '2MT' 2-6-0 No 46443 with the 1.40pm train to Highley. Foley Park Halt was situated here on the right from 1905 to 1925, and on the left from 1925 to 1970. *Andrew Bell*

Left: Situated on the long downhill section from Foley Park to Bewdley is Bewdley Tunnel, 486 yards long, which pierces the sandstone ridge separating the Stour and Severn valleys. On 3 March 2010 LNER Gresley 'K4' Class 2-6-0 No 61994 *The Great Marquess* emerges from the tunnel with a photographic charter special train of BR Mark 1 coaches in 'carmine and cream' livery. As LNER No 3442, *The Great Marquess* was built at Darlington in 1938, one of six specifically designed for service on Scotland's West Highland line, appropriate in this rather wild and wintry view. *Alan Corfield*

Right: Climbing the 1 in 100 gradient to Bewdley Tunnel with gusto is another type of locomotive seen on the West Highland line – LMSR Stanier Class '5MT' 4-6-0 No 5000, later No 45000 in BR days. Crewe-built in 1935, the engine is bringing empty Mark 1 coaches from Bewdley to Kidderminster for the first departure of the day on 30 October 1988. The gorse of the Rifle Range nature reserve looks at its best on this beautiful morning. *Bob Green*

The view from Birchen Coppice escarpment, across the fields of Droppingwells Farm and the nature reserve of the Devil's Spittleful, with Bewdley and the Clee Hills as a backdrop, prove irresistible to train photographers through the seasons. On 8 March 2009 legendary LNER Gresley 'A4' 4-6-2 No 60007 *Sir Nigel Gresley* of 1937, in the BR blue livery of the early 1950s, surges up the gradient with the SVR's set of LNER Gresley coaches. The train is the 1.55pm Bridgnorth to Kidderminster service. *Ralph Ward*

The prospect from the escarpment was rather different one year later, on 24 February 2010. A severe cold spell saw snow-covered fields and frost-laden trees, but GWR 'Manor' Class 4-6-0 No 7802 *Bradley Manor* was well up to the task, powering the 3.08 Highley to Kidderminster dining train on the last lap of the journey. *Bob Green*

This spread shows some classic Great Western Railway locomotives at Bewdley Tunnel.

Left: The Royal Train, conveying TRH The Prince of Wales and The Duchess of Cornwall on a journey along the Severn Valley Railway, drifts down from the tunnel on 10 June 2008, a glorious summer's day. Motive power is provided by Collett 'King' Class 4-6-0 No 6024 *King Edward I*, built at Swindon in 1930. The heavy train is formed of nine BR Mark 3 coaches in Royal Claret livery, all built or adapted for Royal Train service in the period 1977-90. *Chris Wright*

Below left: From heavy trains to light trains! Collett '4575' Class 2-6-2 tank No 5526 bustles towards the tunnel with a Bewdley to Kidderminster 'push and pull' service on 20 September 2008. The engines numbered in the 45xx and 55xx series were popularly known as 'small Prairie tanks'. *Neville Wellings*

Right: The famous one: in 1904 Churchward 'City' Class 4-4-0 locomotive No 3717 *City of Truro*, newly built at Swindon, was credited with reaching a speed of 102mph in Somerset. The exact speed has since been disputed, but it certainly was very, very fast, and earned the locomotive a well-deserved place in the National Collection at York. After years out of use in various museums, the SVR restored the engine, by then No 3440, to active service at Bridgnorth in 1985, followed by a skilled repaint of its elaborate livery at Bewdley. Here, on 17 October 2008, footplateman Bob Heath is enjoying his experience on the engine. It is at the head of a photographers' charter train of appropriate historic coaches from the GWR (SVR) Association's collection. The leading vehicle is 'Siphon G' milk van No 1257. *Peter Quilley*

Left: The gradient from the one-time Bewdley South Junction to the tunnel is a popular place to photograph trains, as we have already seen. GWR Collett 'Hall' Class 4-6-0 No 4936 *Kinlet Hall*, Swindon-built in 1929, forges up the hill with a train of GWR Collett coaching stock on 8 October 2009. *Alan Corfield*

Below left: The Great Storm of 19 June 2007 caused the line in the Severn Valley to be breached in many places, and for a period trains ran between Kidderminster and Bewdley only. The National Collection's LNER Gresley 'V2' Class 2-6-2 No 4771 (BR No 60800) *Green Arrow* had already been booked for a visit from York before the emergency, and thus its operations were confined to a mere 3½ miles. Looking absolutely right heading the LNER Gresley set, the soft syncopated beat of the 'V2' provides an unfamiliar sound at Rifle Range on 22 September 2007. *Peter Marsh*

Right: The bridge over the farm track known as Sandy Lane that once linked Blackstone Farm and Sutton Farm across the Devil's Spittleful is the setting for this view. The Kidderminster to Bridgnorth train crossing it is headed by London, Brighton & South Coast Railway 'E4' Class 0-6-2 tank No 473 *Birch Grove*, here in BR guise as No 32473. This 'Billinton Radial' tank engine, built at Brighton in 1898, is making one of its rare forays away from its home at Sheffield Park, East Sussex, on 18 March 2005. *Peter Marsh*

Right: A Christmas card scene is created near the Devil's Spittleful nature reserve on 9 January 2010. GWR 'Manor' Class 4-6-0 No 7812 *Erlestoke Manor* gallops downhill with the 1.40pm Kidderminster to Highley train formed of BR Mark 1 maroon stock, providing a close resemblance to a Cambrian main line train of the early 1960s. It is passing in front of the site of Rifle Range Halt, which was a timber construction with a 'pagoda'-style hut that served army training camps hereabouts from 1905 until 1920. *Alan Corfield*

GREAT WESTERN RAILWAY.
NOTICE.
ALL PERSONS ARE WARNED NOT TO TRESPASS UPON THE LINES OF RAILWAY OF THE COMPANY, AND NOTICE IS HEREBY GIVEN THAT PURSUANT TO THE PROVISIONS OF THE COMPANY'S ACTS EVERY PERSON WHO TRESPASSES UPON ANY OF THE LINES OF RAILWAY RENDERS HIMSELF LIABLE TO A PENALTY OF FORTY SHILLINGS, AND IN DEFAULT OF PAYMENT TO ONE MONTH'S IMPRISONMENT FOR EVERY SUCH OFFENCE
BY ORDER.

Above: A photo charter train on 19 November 2004 provided a good opportunity to run a credible Great Western Railway local train of the late 1940s period – indeed, creating an authentic 'Severn Valley Railway Journey'. In lovely evening light, Great Western Railway Collett '5101' Class 2-6-2 tank No

5164 accelerates out of the cutting at Bewdley South during an arranged 'run past'. No 5164 was built at Swindon in 1930, and is a prolific member of the SVR's fleet of locos. The three coaches were also Swindon-built, in 1912-23. *Peter Marsh*

Left: There is no disguising the 1 in 100 gradient near the bridge above Bewdley bypass. This evening scene shows GWR Churchward '4500' Class 2-6-2 tank No 4566 lifting the last Bridgnorth to Kidderminster train of the day away from the trees of the Spring Grove estate on 25 October 2010. No 4566 was built at Swindon in 1924, and is nowadays part of the regular SVR roster. Next to the engine is one of the two GWR Hawksworth observation saloons on the SVR. *Malcolm Ranieri*

Above: Bustling out of Bewdley with the 2.02pm Bridgnorth to Kidderminster train is GWR Collett '5101' Class 2-6-2 tank engine No 4160, built at Swindon in 1948. This 'large Prairie tank', as the class is often called, is normally to be found at Minehead, Somerset, but was a visitor to the Autumn Steam Gala on 23 September 2011. The coaches are all from the Churchward and Collett eras on the GWR. *Phil Jones*

Left: The original 1862 route of the Severn Valley Railway to Stourport-on-Severn and Hartlebury Junction is visible in the foreground of this view; it is now a short engineers' siding. The train here, a BR Mark 1 formation headed by BR Standard Class '2MT' 2-6-0 No 78019, is diverging onto the 'Kidderminster Loop' line of 1878, all 3½ miles of which is now part of the heritage Severn Valley Railway. The Riddles-era 2-6-0 was built at Darlington in 1954 and is based at Loughborough, Leicestershire. The 'Cambrian Coast Express' headboard being carried on 7 March 2010 is an authentic fitment, for several of these engines were allocated to Machynlleth in the 1950s and worked the Pwllheli portion of the 'CCE'. *Alan Corfield*

Right: This view was taken on the 10-arch, 101-yard-long Bewdley South, or Sandbourne, Viaduct, with the trees of Spring Grove estate on the right. GWR Collett 'Castle' Class 4-6-0 No 5029 *Nunney Castle*, built at Swindon in 1934, is at the head of a special train comprising mostly Collett coaches of the same era as the engine. The date is 13 March 2009. *Jason Houlders*

A goods train specially chartered by enthusiasts leaves Bewdley via the short Sandbourne cutting on 14 March 2005 under the guiding hand of Driver Jason Houlders. Motive power is provided by Hawksworth-designed '1600' Class lightweight 0-6-0 pannier tank No 1638, normally to be found in passenger service at Rolvenden, Kent. No 1638 represents the final design of GWR pannier tank, actually built under BR auspices at Swindon in 1951. *Peter Marsh*

Bewdley

Here is a general view showing the signalling arrangements at Bewdley South as Caledonian Railway McIntosh '812' Class 0-6-0 No 828 passes the signal box with a Bridgnorth to Kidderminster train on 25 March 2012. The hill known as Maypole Piece rises behind the box. *Bob Green*

Left: This clear view of Bewdley South signal box features GWR 'Manor' 4-6-0 No 7812 *Erlestoke Manor* arriving at Bewdley with the 5.00pm Kidderminster to Bridgnorth train of GWR stock on 24 March 2012. Spring Grove woodland forms the backdrop to the scene. *Alan Corfield*

Below: Former London & North Western Railway 'Super D' Class '7F' 0-8-0 No 49395 eases out of Bewdley station with a Bridgnorth to Kidderminster train on 23 September 2006. This locomotive was built at Crewe in 1921 as LNWR No 485, later becoming LMSR No 9395. The robust Bowen-Cooke design was clearly intended for freight service, but summer use on excursion passenger trains in South Wales was not uncommon. *Joe Dryburgh*

Below: A Bewdley scene of yesteryear features Great Western Railway '5700' Class 0-6-0 pannier tank No 5764 leaving from Platform 2 for Kidderminster on 19 September 2008, pulling a set of passenger coaches from the same company and the same era as the locomotive. This is the 3.31pm from Arley to Kidderminster train. Other GWR equipment completes the scene: a 'Toad' guard's brake van, a 'parachute' water tank, and lower-quadrant signals. No 5764 is a member of the SVR home fleet. It was built at Swindon in 1929, an early member of a class of 863 locomotives, and finished its service with London Transport at Neasden in 1971. *Chris Wright*

Right: Here we move to Bewdley's platforms to view the 12.35pm train from Bridgnorth to Kidderminster arriving in Platform 2. It is headed by GWR Hawksworth-designed '1500' Class 0-6-0 pannier tank No 1501 on 2 August 2003. This outside-cylindered engine is the only survivor of ten built at Swindon in 1949 for operation in yards and sidings with sharp curvature. In practice, most of them were used on empty coaching stock movements at London's Paddington station. *Raymond Jones*

The visit of a Great Western Railway auto-train to the SVR is always a popular event, particularly amongst photographers. On 15 April 2013 GWR Collett '1400' Class 0-4-2 tank No 1450 and auto-coach No W238W *Chaffinch* 'play to the gallery' with a photographers' charter special at Bewdley. The picturesque station was opened in 1862, and extensively modified in 1878 for the opening of the 'Kidderminster Loop'. No 1450 is a Swindon product of 1935. *Alan Corfield*

Another photo charter special to select Bewdley station as a location occurred on 15 October 2012. Southern Railway Maunsell-designed 'U' Class 2-6-0 No 31806 worked from Bridgnorth to Kidderminster with a short train, the ensemble being reminiscent of a train on the erstwhile Midland & South Western Junction line from Cheltenham to Andover. The train is crossing the eight-arch 112-yard-long Bewdley North, or Wribbenhall, Viaduct, with Bewdley North signal box on the left. *Andrew Bell*

Left: Here is a very special occasion! To celebrate 150 years of the Severn Valley Railway in 2012, a suitably ancient steam locomotive was procured. On 14 May, Furness Railway 0-4-0 No 20, originally built in 1863, pulls into the red-brick Bewdley station with a special train from Kidderminster conveying HRH The Duke of Gloucester, the SVR's patron. The coach is GWR Hawksworth Inspection Saloon W80972W of 1948. Station staff provided a guard of honour on Platform 1. *David Wilcock*

The medieval rooftops of Bewdley town provide an interesting foreground to this distant view of the Severn Valley Railway running northwards from Bewdley. LMSR Stanier Class '5MT' 2-6-0 No 42968 leaves Wribbenhall Viaduct and addresses the 1 in 145 climb to Northwood with a 'Santa Special' from Kidderminster to Arley on 23 December 2012. *Phil Jones*

Bewdley to Arley

Left: This scene harks back to the Severn Valley trains of 80 years ago. Great Western Railway '4500' Class 2-6-2 tank No 4566 rounds the long curve alongside Northwood Lane, Bewdley, with a Kidderminster to Arley 'Santa Special' on 18 December 2012. However, most Severn Valley trains of yesteryear were three coaches long, not six! *Ken Woolley*

Right: A little further north, passing Bewdley North's home signal, GWR Collett '5600' Class 0-6-2 tank No 5637, Swindon-built in 1925, casts an impressive shadow over the cutting side. Usually based at Cranmore, Somerset, the engine is heading the 3.36pm Bewdley to Arley service during the Spring Steam Gala on 16 March 2003. *Peter Marsh*

Left: Here is a view across the peaceful River Severn showing GWR '4500' Class 2-6-2 tank No 4566 passing Northwood House on 10 March 2007 with a Bewdley to Bridgnorth train during the Spring Steam Gala.

Right: Christmas Eve, 24 December 2009, finds the Severn Valley coated in a blanket of snow, with frost covering the trees. The location here is alongside Northwood Lane, at the point where the track formation of the Wyre Forest line to Tenbury Wells and Woofferton leaves the Severn Valley line, a mile north of Bewdley station. SVR-based LMSR Ivatt-designed Class '4MT' 2-6-0 No 43106, built at Darlington in 1951, heads a Kidderminster to Arley 'Santa Special' train. It is composed of the SVR-based set of LNER Gresley coaches, a combination found in East Anglia throughout the 1950s on the late-lamented Midland & Great Northern Joint Line.
Alan Corfield

Left: The GWR Hawksworth '9400' Class 0-6-0 pannier tanks were officially banned from working over the Severn Valley line in GWR and BR days, but roving No 9466 of 1952 looks very much at home with a matching set of coaches on 24 September 2005. This train, the 3.30pm from Bridgnorth to Kidderminster, is at the spot where the Wyre Forest line curved away at a lower level to Dowles Bridge. The expanse of the forest known as North Wood forms the backdrop. *Raymond Jones*

Right: Two local ramblers hail an afternoon Bridgnorth to Kidderminster train at Northwood Halt on 25 October 2010, during a particularly colourful autumn leaf-fall period. LMSR Ivatt-designed Class '4MT' 2-6-0 No 43106 is heading the train. The Halt was open from 1935 until 1963 and again from 1974 until the present day. It only acquired the GWR waiting shelter with its distinctive 'pagoda'-style roof in 2006. *Ralph Ward*

Here is the westernmost of the two Trimpley reservoirs, built between 1964 and 1968, with the expanse of Eymore Wood rising to form an impressive backdrop. Not visible in the foreground is the River Severn, skirting the reservoirs at a lower level, although trees on the lower reaches of Seckley Wood are just in the frame. LMSR Ivatt Class '4MT' No 43106 and its southbound train of BR standard Mark 1 coaches in 'carmine and cream' livery provide a toylike element in this 3 December 2011 scene. *Andrew Bell*

Bewdley to Arley

The perfect view of an approaching train! GWR Collett '5101' Class 2-6-2 tank No 5164 tackles the curving 1 in 145 climb through the deep Eymore Wood cutting on 5 April 2009. The rear of this Bridgnorth to Kidderminster train will just be leaving the span of Victoria Bridge, and passengers will very soon be sighting the westernmost of the Trimpley reservoirs.
Alan Corfield

Left: The classic view of Victoria Bridge from the south-west has been a powerful tool in publicity for the Severn Valley Railway during the preservation era. LMSR Fowler 'Standard' Class '3F' 0-6-0 tank No 47406 crosses the 200-foot-long clear span on the bright afternoon of 23 March 2012, at the head of a Highley to Bewdley service during the Spring Steam Gala. Loughborough-based No 47406 was built at Vulcan Foundry in 1926, one of 422 of this class in BR service, which were known as 'Jinties' by the vast majority of enthusiasts. No 47383 of the class was a regular in SVR service until it entered The Engine House in 2008. *Bob Green*

Right: GWR Collett 'King' Class 4-6-0 No 6024 *King Edward I* drifts across Victoria Bridge with a Kidderminster to Bridgnorth party special train on 15 November 2009. Beyond the bridge the trees of Eymore Wood have changed colour, and the heights of the Trimpley area dominate the skyline. *Bob Green*

Left: GWR Collett 'Manor' Class 4-6-0 No 7812 *Erlestoke Manor* makes a crossing of Victoria Bridge that produces a surprisingly clear reflection in the flowing waters of the Severn. The train is a Kidderminster to Bridgnorth working on 24 March 2012. Victoria Bridge was the longest cast-iron clear span in the world when completed in 1861, opening only shortly before an almost identical structure, the Albert Edward Bridge at Ironbridge, was completed. This also is still in use, carrying diesel-hauled coal trains. *Phil Jones*

Right: This view has been extensively used in SVR publicity in recent years, but deserves its place in this book. Eymore Wood trees are in almost full foliage as GWR Collett 'Hall' Class 4-6-0 No 4930 *Hagley Hall* heads up the short gradient from Victoria Bridge to Arley station with the Bridgnorth-bound 'Severn Valley Limited' dining train on 23 September 1984. No 4930 was built at Swindon in 1929. *Bob Green*

Below: The bright snowy morning of 19 December 2010 finds GWR Collett 'Manor' 4-6-0 No 7802 *Bradley Manor* leaving the Great Cutting south of Arley with a 'Santa Special' for Kidderminster. The weather conditions were difficult, but a full SVR train service was maintained during the day. Back in 1861 several navvies were badly injured during the excavation of this cutting. *Bob Green*

Right: Shades of Beattock? LMSR Stanier 'Princess Coronation' Class "8P" 4-6-2 No 6233 *Duchess of Sutherland* disturbs the peace of the valley lifting her northbound 11-coach train up the 1 in 180 gradient from Victoria Bridge to Arley station. On this misty 23 September 2006 the division between Eymore Wood (left) and Seckley Wood (right) is discernible above the train, and Trimpley reservoirs and the River Severn occupy this chasm. No 6233 – later BR No 46233 – was built at Crewe in 1938 and is a representative of the most powerful main-line passenger steam locomotive class in Britain. Here she is running on little more than half-power! *Alan Corfield*

Arley

Southern Railway 'USA' Class 0-6-0 tank No 65 – later BR No 30065 – enters Arley station through the Great Cutting with two LMSR coaches forming the 11.25am Kidderminster to Arley local service on 24 March 2013. This was the snowiest of Spring Steam Galas ever experienced by the SVR, although the train service was maintained and passengers who managed to reach the Railway were richly rewarded by the experience. No 65 was built in 1943 at Vulcan Iron Works, Wilkes-Barre, Pennsylvania, USA, for European war theatre service. Changed circumstances meant that it was amongst many examples stored in Britain, latterly at Newbury. It was rescued as one of 14 of the type bought by the Southern Railway in 1947 for service in Southampton Docks. In preservation, it is one of a pair based at Rolvenden, Kent. *Bob Sweet*

Another popular visitor from the Rolvenden stable was London, Brighton & South Coast Railway 'A1X' Class 'Terrier' 0-6-0 tank No 32678, here seen working the 5.01pm goods train to Bewdley at Arley station on 19 September 2003. Built at Brighton in 1880 as No 78 *Knowle*, this iconic locomotive started life as a South London suburban passenger engine, later spending 7 years on the Isle of Wight as No W4 *Bembridge*, before finishing its BR service at Newhaven Harbour in 1963. Butlins Holiday Camp at Minehead saved the engine from the cutter's torch before a return to its natural home in rural Kent beckoned. *Raymond Jones*

Right: This viewpoint emphasises the large-diameter chimney of Southern rebuilt 'West Country' Class 4-6-2 No 34027 *Taw Valley*, here running in disguise as scrapped classmate No 34045 *Ottery St Mary*, on 12 July 2004. This view of the 11.00am Bridgnorth to Kidderminster train at Platform 1 of the yellow-brick Arley station was recorded from the stone bridge carrying the lane from Button Oak, in the Wyre Forest, to the river ferry landing. The ferry service here terminated upon the opening of a footbridge across the river in 1973. The passing loop and Platform 2 were added in 1883, some 21 years after the station's opening. *Eddie Johnson*

Right: Arley station is shown clearly in this view of a photographers' charter goods train working 'wrong line' through Platform 1 on 30 March 2012. Motive power is provided by home-based GWR Churchward '2800' Class 2-8-0 No 2857, built at Swindon in 1918, and the train is composed of GWR goods wagons typical of the engine's era. The running lines and Platform 2 in the foreground had only recently been rebuilt as part of a major drainage replacement scheme. *Alan Corfield*

Left: A Severn Valley scene of yesteryear was recreated at Arley station during a photo charter session on the misty morning of 13 January 2006. GWR Collett '5700' Class 0-6-0 pannier tank No 5764 performs a 'run past' through Platform 1, hauling a pair of GWR coaches of the same era as the locomotive. The only obvious change from the 1930s here is the 'alien' LNWR-type signal box, moved from Yorton near Whitchurch, which opened here in 1976 and replaced the original GWR box, demolished in 1967. *Peter Marsh*

Right: A grandstand view of Arley station presents itself from the cutting immediately to the north. Perfect combustion is evident as GWR Collett 'Manor' Class 4-6-0 No 7802 *Bradley Manor* restarts the eight-coach 3.45pm Kidderminster to Bridgnorth train on the 1 in 180 gradient on 1 May 2005. Arley station actually serves the village on the opposite bank of the river, which is known as Upper Arley! *Raymond Jones*

Arley to Highley

Left: Arley north cutting disappears to reveal the sloping pasture below Skeet's Farm. The northern extent of the Wyre Forest borders the line in the left background, while the trees behind the train shield views of the river for much of the year. The main focus of attention in this scene is LMSR Stanier Class '5MT' 4-6-0 No 45110 hauling a photographers' charter train southbound on 27 April 1999. Specially included in the train is the LMSR Stanier full brake van No M31420M in BR carmine livery, nowadays usually in static use at Kidderminster carriage works. No 45110 was built by Vulcan Foundry, Newton-le-Willows, Lancashire, in 1935, and hauled the last BR passenger train of the steam era in 1968. Between 1970 and 2008 it ran 107,000 miles on the SVR. *Peter Marsh*

Right: A really classic LMSR locomotive is Stanier 'Princess Royal' Class '8P' 4-6-2 No 6201 *Princess Elizabeth*, seen here leaving Arley in immaculate condition with the 12.30pm Kidderminster to Bridgnorth train of matching LMSR coaches in crimson lake livery on 21 September 2002. No 6201 was built at Crewe in 1933, the second of 13 of a class that immediately revolutionised the fastest train services between London Euston and Glasgow Central. It became No 46201 in the BR era after 1948. The area forming the background to this scene was the southern extremity of Staffordshire for many years, appropriate for this class of locomotive, but it is now part of Worcestershire. *Raymond Jones*

Above: British Railways Standard Class '8P' 4-6-2 No 71000 *Duke of Gloucester* creates a memorable sight thanks to the dramatic lighting conditions of 7 March 2009. The locomotive is accelerating from Arley with the 2.05pm Kidderminster to Bridgnorth train during the Spring Steam Gala. Reflections off the wheel rims bear testimony to the exhibition finish of this three-cylindered machine with its Caprotti valve gear. Built at Crewe in 1954, it was the last new express passenger steam locomotive type in Britain, the design never being perpetuated with further examples. *Jason Houlders*

Right: One of the finest views of the Severn Valley and its railway is obtainable just north of Severn Lodge, midway between Arley and Highley. GWR Churchward '2800' Class 2-8-0 No 2857 heads northwards with a photographers' charter goods train on 30 March 2012. This rural scene was disfigured a little between 1880 and 1943 when Kinlet Sidings existed here. They were controlled by a signal box from 1913 onwards, sited at the junction of a branch line that threaded the valley of the Borle Brook, bringing coal down from Billingsley and Kinlet collieries. *Phil Jones*

Above: The solitude of the valley at Kinlet is briefly disturbed by the passage of a southbound train headed by GWR 'Manor' Class 4-6-0 No 7812 *Erlestoke Manor* on 25 September 2010. This wide view from the hills above the east bank of the River Severn near Hextons Farm only illuminates trains strongly in the mornings. On this occasion the Clee Hills are clearly visible on the horizon. Vegetation around the tree on the right masks a glimpse of Borle Viaduct. *Bob Green*

Right: But here is a close-up view of Borle Viaduct! This four-arch structure spans the Borle Brook tributary just 50 yards from its confluence with the River Severn. It is being crossed in vigorous fashion by Caledonian Railway '812' Class 0-6-0 No 828 heading a southbound charter train of three LMSR Stanier coaches on 3 October 2011. The scene here is reminiscent of parts of Ayrshire in south-west Scotland, where the engine was a familiar sight for most of its 64-year working life. *Phil Jones*

The 2.40pm local service from Kidderminster to Highley leaves Stanley cutting and approaches its destination during the Autumn Steam Gala on 25 September 2009. Heading the Great Western train of three Collett coaches and 'Siphon G' van No 1257 is Port Talbot Railway 0-6-0 saddle tank No 26, originally built by contractors Hudswell Clarke at Leeds in 1901. The engine was later 'Great Westernised', and is preserved in this rebuilt condition as GWR No 813. The fourth locomotive to arrive on the SVR at Bridgnorth in 1967, since restoration it has toured Britain extensively while on hire to heritage railways and centres. *David C. Williams*

The South Wales theme continues with this view of GWR Collett '5600' Class 0-6-2 tank No 6695, built by Armstrong Whitworth at Newcastle in 1928. Two hundred of these engines were built, the majority being stationed in the South Wales valleys, pulling coal trains – as seen here – to the coastal marshalling yards and dockyards. No 6695 is today based at Swanage, and is preserved in the attractive lined green livery applied to some members of the class by British Railways in the late 1950s. The locomotive is approaching Highley from the south on 5 March 2010. *Peter Marsh*

Highley

Left: Only in bright sunlight does the magnificent dark blue livery applied to some Somerset & Dorset Joint Railway locomotives show to advantage. Here Fowler Derby-designed Darlington-built Class '7F' 2-8-0 No 88, eventually BR No 53808, approaches Highley with the 3.00pm Kidderminster to Bridgnorth train on 22 March 2008. Eleven of these impressive engines were stationed at Bath depot for working goods trains over the Mendip Hills. No 88 remains in Somerset, but is based nowadays at Minehead. *Raymond Jones*

Above: A further reminder of the Somerset & Dorset line comes in the form of Southern Railway Bulleid 'Battle of Britain' Class 4-6-2 No 34070 *Manston*, seen approaching Highley with the 1.50pm Kidderminster to Bridgnorth train on 25 September 2010. Five members of the identical 'West Country' Class were allocated to Bath from 1951 until 1955, and others served on the route for a further seven years. Today No 34070 is Dorset-based, at Swanage. These contrasting seasonal views were taken from the balcony of The Engine House, the SVR visitor centre that opened in 2008. *Raymond Jones*

On these pages are scenes at the south end of Highley station, which is actually located in the hamlet of Stanley.

Above: Viewed from the 2009-built footbridge, GWR Churchward '4500' Class 2-6-2 tank No 4566 passes the cattle dock as it arrives with the 2.15pm Kidderminster to Bridgnorth train on 22 May 2010. In the background is The Engine House visitor centre. *John Oates*

Right: GWR Collett 'Manor' Class 4-6-0 No 7812 *Erlestoke Manor* leaves with the 2.55pm Bridgnorth to Kidderminster train on 26 May 2012, viewed from the footpath to The Engine House. *Raymond Jones*

Below: Seen from The Engine House entrance, LMR Ivatt Class '4MT' 2-6-0 No 43106 passes Highley with the SVR's Fortieth Anniversary special train on 23 May 2010. *Bob Sweet*

Below right: LMSR Stanier Class '5MT' 2-6-0 No 42968 leaves with a Bridgnorth to Kidderminster service on Boxing Day, 26 December 2010, during blizzard conditions at Highley. *Bob Sweet*

Right: A panorama looking northwards from the footbridge at the stone-built Highley station on 3 September 2012 shows Southern Railway rebuilt 'Battle of Britain' Class 4-6-2 No 34053 *Sir Keith Park* arriving to brisk business with the 2.55pm Bridgnorth to Kidderminster train. A second passenger platform was planned around 1887 but never built, unfortunately for the present-day SVR. Thus coal traffic from Highley and Alveley collieries continued to play the major role operationally until preservation days, and the passenger station was never enlarged. *John Oates*

Above: The northbound departure from Highley is by a sharp curve leading immediately to a 1 in 100 gradient that can tax smaller locomotives on heavier trains, particularly during poor weather conditions. There is no problem here for LMSR Stanier Class '5MT' 4-6-0 No 45110 as it leaves with the 3.00pm Kidderminster to Bridgnorth train on 19 June 2004. *Raymond Jones*

Highley to Hampton Loade

Three-quarters of a mile north of Highley station lies the unstaffed Country Park Halt, newly built in 1996. It serves the nearby Severn Valley Country Park and was funded through a Bridgnorth District Council grant. It is situated on the site of part of Alveley Colliery sidings, which closed in 1969. The 1.35pm Bridgnorth to Kidderminster train headed by GWR Collett 'Manor' Class 4-6-0 No 7812 *Erlestoke Manor* calls at the halt on 1 August 2013. *John Oates*

The line north of Country Park Halt runs into Alveley's woodlands, with only the briefest glimpses of the River Severn to the east in summertime. Just half a mile south of Hampton Loade, nearing Londonderry Coppice, views of the river open up. Visiting from its base at Ropley, Hampshire, British Railways Standard Class '5MT' 4-6-0 No 73096 heads the 11.30am Kidderminster to Bridgnorth train on 20 September 2003. No 73096 was among the last steam engines built in Britain, at Derby in 1955, to a design by R. A. Riddles. *Raymond Jones*

Turning around from the previous picture, here is the view looking towards Hampton Loade station on a glorious day. GWR 'Collett Goods' or '2251' Class 0-6-0 No 3205 gets into its stride with the 1.55pm Bridgnorth to Highley train on 25 September 2010. On the extreme right can be glimpsed the River Severn, while the foreground is occupied by National Cycle Route 45, which will link Chester with Salisbury and occupies a strip of land within the boundary of SVR property for more than a mile in this vicinity. No 3205, built at Swindon in 1946, became memorably the first locomotive to arrive at Bridgnorth in preservation on 25 March 1967. It is now based at Bucfastleigh, Devon *Alan Corfield*

It is difficult to believe that the views on this spread actually depict the same engine in the same place! GWR Collett '5101' class 2-6-2 tank No 5164 is seen proceeding southwards just a few hundred yards south of Hampton Loade station.

Above: The 'large Prairie' is seen here from the riverbank on a warm 12 April 2009, heading the 12.40pm Bridgnorth to Kidderminster train. Note the railway boundary fence on the left of the picture, which constrains the cycle route path where it needs to rise to remain within SVR property – technically known as a 'pinch point'. *Paul Pearson*

Right: A demonstration goods train, chartered by railway photographers and also headed by No 5164, approaches the 'gallery' on 21 April 2013. The train provides an accurate evocation of a Severn Valley line goods service of the 1940s. Underhill Coppice forms the backdrop on the opposite bank of the river. *Phil Jones*

Hampton Loade

Hampton Loade station is located in the hamlet of Hampton and was originally named simply that! The hamlet of Hampton Loade is actually across the river, reached by a chain-driven ferry conveying passengers only. From 1862 the station comprised only a single platform, until the loop was added in 1883.

Left: The Southern comes to Hampton Loade! Maunsell-designed 'U' Class 2-6-0 No 31806 performs a 'run past' for photographers through Platform 1 on 15 October 2012, passing the massed ranks of milk churns awaiting collection on the later-added Platform 2. In this scene the signal box, being repainted, is switched out of use, all trains using Platform 1. Behind the engine is Southern PLV parcels van No 1174 in malachite green livery and four BR coaches in 'carmine and cream' livery, forming a fair impression of a Midland & South Western Junction Railway Andover to Cheltenham train of the 1950s. The engine was built to a South Eastern & Chatham Railway design of 1917 as 'K' Class 2-6-4 tank No A806

River Torridge at Ashford, Kent, in 1926, and converted to a 2-6-0 tender engine at Brighton in 1928. The PLV van was also built at Ashford, in 1935. *Andrew Bell*

Above: The length and livery of the train betray that this is not a genuine scene from the 1930s. GWR Churchward '4500' Class 2-6-2 tank locomotive No 4566 calls at the yellow-brick Hampton Loade station with a seven-coach train of BR Mark 1 stock forming the 12.20pm service from Kidderminster to Bridgnorth on 31 May 2012. *John Oates*

Left: Great Western Railway '2251' Class 0-6-0 No 3205 rumbles over the bridge that spans the lane linking Chelmarsh with Hampton ferry landing. The cottage in the view, which is located opposite the main entrance to Hampton Loade station, dates from the 18th century, thus predating the arrival of the railway here. No 3205 is at the head of a short train of goods vans forming a photographic charter special on 9 May 2000. *Peter Marsh*

Right: A view from the other side of the line provides an impressive angle on LMSR Stanier Class '8F' 2-8-0 No 48773 as it enters the station with the 11.57am Bridgnorth to Kidderminster train on 15 March 2003. As LMSR No 8233, the locomotive was built by the North British Locomotive Company at Glasgow in 1940, and soon requisitioned for war service in the Middle East, not returning to Britain until 1952. The engine then served on the Longmoor Military Railway in Hampshire, and on British Railways from 1957 until 1968. During preservation on the SVR, it became the highest mileage loco, and had achieved 151,000 miles by early 2008. *Peter Marsh*

Hampton Loade to Eardington

This pair of pictures was taken from the hillside below New House Farm, Chelmarsh, between Hampton Loade and Eardington. Looking southwards, the eyes are assaulted by the sight of London & North Eastern Railway Gresley 'A4' Class 4-6-2 No 4464 *Bittern* in garter blue livery at the head of seven contemporary LNER Gresley teak coaches from the SVR-based fleet. This is a photographers' charter special on 26 March 2012, recreating a credible LNER East Coast Main Line express train of the late 1930s.

No 4464 was built at Doncaster in 1937, and was based at Gateshead, Tyneside, until spending an Indian Summer of activity based at Aberdeen until 1966 as BR No 60019. On the opposite bank of the River Severn in the background is the woodland strip known as Long Covert, the trees still bare at this time of year. *Phil Jones*

Looking northwards, an equally rewarding view was available on 25 September 2010, but in this case it was a public passenger train operating during the Autumn Steam Gala. LMSR Stanier 'Jubilee' Class 5XP – later 6P – 4-6-0 No 5690 *Leander* heads, a seven-coach rake of matching LMSR Stanier coaches from the SVR-based fleet, the 1.28pm from Bridgnorth to Kidderminster. This is a credible West Coast Main Line, or Midland Main Line, express train of the late 1930s, completely in crimson lake livery. No 5690 was built at Crewe in 1936, and withdrawn from service as BR No 45690 at Bristol in 1964. The National Trust property of Dudmaston Hall, within its woodland estate displaying autumnal colours, is just visible behind the locomotive's exhaust. *Alan Corfield*

Left: To complete the three pre-nationalisation train liveries photographed below New House Farm, here is the one that is entirely appropriate to the Severn Valley line. Great Western Railway Collett '5101' Class 2-6-2 tank No 5164 recovers from the 15mph restriction at Sterns with the eight-coach 1.40pm Bridgnorth to Kidderminster train on 24 September 2004. Six of the coaches are also GWR Collett vehicles, the exceptions being the GWR Hawksworth and BR Mark 1 coaches that are respectively second and fifth in the formation. However, the vehicles all harmonise well in chocolate and cream livery. *Raymond Jones*

Above right: A visitor to the Autumn Steam Gala in 2005 was GWR Hawksworth-designed 'Modified Hall' or '6959' Class 4-6-0 No 7903 *Foremarke Hall*, which was actually completed in BR days at Swindon in 1949. On 23 September the immaculate engine accelerates away from the Sterns speed restriction with a Kidderminster to Bridgnorth train formed of some of the SVR's GWR coaches. *Raymond Jones*

Below right: At the same spot another visitor, Southern Railway Maunsell 'Schools' or 'V' Class 4-4-0 No 30926 *Repton* recovers from the slack with the 11.45am train from Kidderminster to Bridgnorth on the unseasonably warm day of 24 September 2004. As Southern Railway No 926, *Repton* was built at Eastleigh and entered service in 1934. The 40 engines of the class were used on all Southern main lines and were popular with enginemen, producing noteworthy performances on the London to Bournemouth, Portsmouth and Hastings routes. After withdrawal in 1962 this engine was domiciled in the USA and Canada from 1966 onwards, returning to these shores and the North Yorkshire Moors Railway in 1989. *Raymond Jones*

Left: A major event in 2009 was the visit of a brand-new steam locomotive to the Severn Valley! The A1 Locomotive Trust's LNER Peppercorn-designed 'A1' Class 4-6-2 No 60163 *Tornado* took 14 years to build and cost more than £3 million. Only one year after completion at Darlington it is united with the appropriate – and genuine! – LNER Gresley coaches of the 11.00am Kidderminster to Bridgnorth train on 25 September. It is leaving Sterns Coppice and effortlessly addressing the 1½-mile climb, mostly graded at 1 in 100, to Eardington summit. The posts alongside the third coach of the train prevent misadventure over the parapet of the bridge spanning the Mor Brook. *Alan Corfield*

Above: At the same location is a train more reminiscent of the Severn Valley line. GWR Collett '5700' Class 0-6-0 pannier tank No 5786 heads the three-coach 3.51pm Highley to Bewdley train during the Spring Steam Gala on 6 March 2010. No 5786 was built at Swindon in 1930 and finished its everyday service with London Transport in 1969. Nowadays it is based at Buckfastleigh in Devon. *Tom Thacker*

Left: The Great Western 'auto-trains' were not particularly associated with the Severn Valley line, but before the introduction of GWR diesel railcars in the 1940s certain short journeys at the south end on the route were operated by small tank engines and single coaches in 'push and pull' mode as 'auto-trains'. Reviving this practice on 24 September 2005 is Collett '1400' Class 0-4-2 tank No 1450 with trailer coach No 178, both Swindon-built, in 1935 and 1930 respectively. The train, normally based in Lydney, is approaching Hay Bridge at the start of a spirited ascent of Eardington bank. *Steve Lewis*

Right: Also making a vigorous attack on Eardington bank is this London & North Western Railway 0-6-2 'Coal Tank', built at Crewe to F. W. Webb's design in 1888. Three hundred of these effective, versatile and economical locomotives ranged over the network of the 'Premier Line' for more than 70 years, from London to Carlisle and Peterborough to Swansea and Holyhead. This engine was LNWR No 1054, LMSR No 7799 (as here) and BR No 58926. During its second visit to the SVR, on 22 September 2012, the '2F' Class engine heads a two-coach Hampton Loade to Bridgnorth train across Hay Bridge. Built by the Brymbo Ironworks, Wrexham, in 1861, this structure spans the B4555 Bridgnorth to Highley road. *Bob Green*

Eardington
(Closed)

Situated in a rural farming area, Eardington station has a chequered railway history. It opened in 1868, was reduced to unstaffed status (but note, not officially a 'Halt') in 1949, and closed with the line in 1963. It opened under preservation in 1970, finally closing to trains in 1982, but is still maintained in good condition by a dedicated team of supporters. The engineers' siding in these views has in the past served as a loop line, and for a period was missing completely.

Right: Southern 'U' Class 2-6-0 No 31806 heads a southbound photographers' charter special on the beautiful morning of 16 October 2012. Eardington bridge in the background carries the B4555 road over the line. *Andrew Bell*

Far right: This wider view of Eardington station site includes the historic brick building containing the booking office and waiting room. Another Southern locomotive, 'T9' Class 4-4-0 No 30120, scurries past the station with a photographers' charter special on 18 October 2012. It was one of 66 locomotives of this long-lived Dugald Drummond design, known as 'Greyhounds', and was built at Nine Elms, London, in 1899. *Tom Clarke*

Eardington bridge, north of the station, provides a superb viewpoint in both directions. Only early in the day does the sun illuminate the southerly scene in this way, showing to good effect LMSR Stanier Class '5MT' 2-6-0 No 42968 as it makes brisk work of the 1 in 100 gradient of Eardington bank with the 9.20am Kidderminster to Bridgnorth train on 22 September 2012. *Alan Castle*

Looking northwards from Eardington bridge, Southern Railway rebuilt 'Battle of Britain' Class 4-6-2 No 34053 *Sir Keith Park* drifts down Eardington bank with the 2.55pm Bridgnorth to Kidderminster train on 1 July 2013. In the centre background beyond the cutting is the memorably named Daddy Wood. Totally out of sight below the locomotive is the defunct Eardington Canal tunnel, which linked the Upper Forge in the Mor Valley to the left with the Lower Forge alongside the River Severn to the right. The 750-yard bore was in use from 1782 to 1889 for the transport of local iron products. *John Oates*

Eardington to Bridgnorth

The views on this spread show the glacial valley north of Eardington, which proved so useful in the construction of the Severn Valley line in the late 1850s, and today provides a natural amphitheatre for train photography.

Great Western Railway 'Dukedog' or '3200' Class 4-4-0 No 3217 drifts down Eardington bank with six GWR coaches forming the 4.10pm Bridgnorth to Kidderminster train on 19 September 2008. Thirty of these locomotives were assembled at Swindon in 1936-39 utilising the boilers of withdrawn 'Duke' 4-4-0s mounted on the frames of

withdrawn 'Bulldog' 4-4-0s, hence the nickname. Their most substantive work was performed in mid-Wales, but they were seen on other GWR lines including this one. As BR No 9017, this was the last survivor of the class in 1960 and is based at Sheffield Park, Sussex. *Neville Wellings*

Another GWR class of locomotive associated with the Severn Valley line was the Churchward '4300' Class 2-6-0, introduced in 1911, but not officially permitted to operate in the valley until 1943. In all, 342 examples of the design were built up to 1932, then in 1936-39 100 engines were withdrawn for conversion and enlargement to 'Grange' and 'Manor' 4-6-0s. After withdrawal, only two survived at Barry scrapyard to be saved. The SVR-based example, No 7325, was completed at Swindon under Collett's aegis in 1932 as No 9303, and features later design improvements. It is here seen tackling the 1 in 100 gradient of Eardington bank on 9 November 1998 with a northbound photographers' charter train. Next to the engine is BR-built cattle van No B891504, one of the last examples of the thousands built during a century of live cattle transportation. *Bob Green*

This page features trains near Eardington summit, which at 210 feet above sea level is the highest point on the line between Kidderminster and Bridgnorth, and indeed between Hartlebury and Shrewsbury if considering the full length of the original SVR.

Left: A timeless Severn Valley preservation scene is shown here. One of the line's highest-mileage locomotives, having achieved 132,000 by 2008, and the second to be received at Bridgnorth in 1967, was LMSR Class '2MT' 2-6-0 No 46443, designed by H. G. Ivatt and built at Crewe in 1950. Here the engine climbs Eardington bank with the 2.30pm Kidderminster to Bridgnorth train on 7 February 2009, a bitterly cold day with snow remaining in the corries. *Alan Corfield*

Below left: A Gresley odyssey presents itself here, the image being taken on the opposite side of the line from the previous picture. Great Northern Railway 0-6-2 tank No 1744 of 1921 (better known as BR 'N2' Class No 69523) makes steady progress to the summit with the 6.30am morning train from Kidderminster to Bridgnorth on 27 September 2009. The train consists of a matching set of Gresley teak coaches, the first, 2701, being Great Northern-built in 1922, the others a decade or so later during the LNER era, but to the same general design. No 1744 is Loughborough-based. *Alan Corfield*

Right: Even running downhill, a British Railways Standard Class '9F' 2-10-0 can look impressive and powerful, being a big and black machine. Between 1954 and 1960 251 of these heavy freight locomotives were built under the design direction of R. A. Riddles at Crewe and Swindon, constituting the final really successful British steam design. One of the last examples, Swindon-built No 92212, heads a southbound demonstration goods train during the Autumn Steam Gala on 24 September 2011. No 92212's home is at Ropley, Hampshire. Eardington summit is just visible through Slade Lane overbridge, sometimes referred to as Crossing Cottage bridge, in the background. *Phil Jones*

Many of the scenes in this volume have a ring of authenticity about them, but none more so than this view of GWR 0-6-0 saddle tank No 813 panting up the final 100 yards to Eardington summit with a demonstration goods train during the

Autumn Steam Gala on 27 September 2009. Quatford Woods forms the distant backdrop on the opposite bank of the River Severn, with the Bridgnorth aluminium factory also visible. *Andy Taylor*

Right: Here we see contrasting weather conditions at Crossing Cottage, Eardington! In the first view British Railways Standard Class '4MT' 2-6-4 tank No 80072 passes the cottage and approaches the summit in confident style with the 2.20pm Kidderminster to Bridgnorth train on 6 April 2013. It will then be largely downhill to the terminus. No 80072 is Llangollen-based, and has spent several periods on loan to the SVR. The line's own example, No 80079, was a high-mileage engine from 1977 to 2002, achieving 103,000 miles until retired to The Engine House, Highley, in 2008. Both locos were Brighton-built in 1953/54 and Essex-based until electrification there in 1962, when 21 locos of the type were transferred to the Western Region, some seeing Severn Valley line service. No 80072 was unique in serving at Leamington Spa for nearly two years. *Ralph Ward*

Far right: At the same place, but viewed from the opposite side of the line, fog was a hazard early on 23 March 2012 when GWR 'Manor' Class 4-6-0 No 7812 *Erlestoke Manor* with Driver Duncan Ballard approached the summit heading the 7.00am Bewdley to Bridgnorth demonstration goods train. Great care has to be exercised by the train crew in such circumstances. *Phil Jones*

Left: Nearing the summit of the 1½-mile climb from Bridgnorth is Great Western Railway '5101' Class 2-6-2 tank No 5164, at the head of the 2.00pm train to Highley on 24 February 2011. The rear of the train is emerging from the short 44-yard-long Knowlesands Tunnel under the B4555 road from Bridgnorth to Highley. *Alan Corfield*

Above: North of Knowlesands Tunnel Southern 'T9' Class 4-4-0 No 30120 is making steady progress up the 1 in 100 gradient from Oldbury Viaduct towards the tunnel with a southbound charter train for photographers on 18 October 2012. *Alan Corfield*

The splendid prospect of the five-arch Oldbury Viaduct, half a mile south of Bridgnorth, fills this scene as a photo charter special makes the crossing on 14 March 2005. At the head is GWR-designed, BR-built Hawksworth '1600' Class lightweight 0-6-0 pannier tank No 1638, and the train consists of two historic GWR coaches, Nos 3930 of 1915 and 9369 of 1923. The earthworks and structures between Bridgnorth and Eardington summit allowed for the double-track formation of an aborted Wolverhampton rail scheme, including the tunnel and this viaduct, as is evident in this view. The manicured parkland of Oldbury Grange occupies the left background and a glimpse of Bridgnorth's High Town is afforded on the horizon to the right. *Peter Marsh*

Above: This album highlights several of the viewpoints used by photographers at the 87-yard-long Oldbury Viaduct. Seen from the lineside on a dull 5 March 2007, GWR Churchward '4500' Class 2-6-2 tank No 4566 sprints across the viaduct with a charter passenger train comprising GWR fruit van No 2303 of 1898 and two Collett coaches. To the left is Bridgnorth's down home signal. *Raymond Jones*

Right: The Spring Steam Gala of 2013 featured unseasonably severe weather conditions. On 26 March, just two days after the Gala weekend, GWR '1400' Class 0-4-2 tank No 1450 crosses the viaduct with auto-coach No W238W *Chaffinch* forming a northbound charter train. In the foreground, coated in snow, is Daniel's Mill, whose waterwheel is visible on the right of the building. This restored flour mill is now a noted tourist attraction in the Bridgnorth district. *Phil Jones*

Left: Here is a final view of Oldbury Viaduct, this time looking east from alongside the supply stream to the watermill, which is visible under the viaduct. Atop the arches on 3 April 2013, Southern Railway Bulleid 'West Country' Class 4-6-2 No 34007 *Wadebridge*, in original form, is making a gentle climb out of Bridgnorth with the 1.35pm train to Kidderminster,

formed of LNER coaches. No 34007 was built at Brighton in 1945 as No 21C107 and withdrawn in 1965. It is now based at Ropley, Hampshire. *Phil Jones*

Above: Nearer to Bridgnorth is Oldbury cutting, and viewed from the site of the old permanent way hut the classic combination of a pair of GWR 'Manor' Class 4-6-0s

fills the view on 26 March 2010. No 7802 *Bradley Manor* leads No 7812 *Erlestoke Manor* southwards in a recreation of the most powerful combination available on the former Cambrian Railways main line in the early 1960s. No 7802 wears the silver-painted embellishments accorded to regularly rostered 'Cambrian Coast Express' engines at Aberystwyth depot. *Peter Marsh*

Left: Emerging from Oldbury cutting at Bridgnorth, and creating a magnificent smoke and steam effect in dramatic lighting conditions, GWR Collett '5700' Class 0-6-0 pannier tank No 7714 heads the 10.20am train to Kidderminster on 18 November 1995. The BR black-liveried locomotive complements the four BR Mark 1 coaches in 'carmine and cream' livery on this winter morning. *Bob Green*

Right: The photographer is standing on Oldbury cutting side at a spot above the train in the last picture. The subject is Southern rebuilt 'Battle of Britain' Class 4-6-2 No 34053 *Sir Keith Park*, leaving Bridgnorth with the 2.00pm train to Kidderminster on 19 February 2013. Clearly visible in this view are the Bridgnorth High Town churches, St Leonard's of 1862 in the centre and the Thomas Telford-designed St Mary Magdalene's of 1792 on the right. *Ralph Ward*

Right: This is a driver's-eye view of the approach to Bridgnorth from the footplate of LNER 'A4' Class 4-6-2 No 60009 *Union of South Africa.* The 'Pacific' locomotive is arriving with the 2.15pm service from Kidderminster on 16 August 2002, and the down inner home signal is indicating that this will be a Platform 1 arrival. A parapet of the bridge over the B4363 road to Cleobury Mortimer is visible beyond the signal. *David C. Williams*

Far right: Here is the conventional view at the 'business end' of Bridgnorth station. LMSR-pattern Ivatt Class '2MT' 2-6-0 No 46443 is being readied for one of the many hundreds of departures that it has made from this station since April 1967, when it arrived here directly from BR ownership in Manchester. This is the six-coach 12.15pm train to Kidderminster on 28 June 2011. *Raymond Jones*

Far left: Contrasting with the previous scene is this evening view of the 7.52pm departure to Kidderminster on 24 September 2011. At the head of the train is GWR Collett 'King' Class 4-6-0 No 6024 *King Edward I*, appropriately sporting the 'Cornish Riviera Express' headboard and the '635' reporting number for that train. *Adam Crick*

Left: Following massive storm damage on 20 June 2007, the Severn Valley line between Bewdley and Bridgnorth was breached in many places. A few weeks later, on 11 August, the only passenger journey possible at the north end of the line was aboard this one-coach shuttle train from Bridgnorth station to Oldbury cutting, half-a-mile away. Power was provided by GWR '5700' Class 0-6-0 pannier tank No 7714. Proceeds from this operation went to the newly created appeal to fund storm recovery. *Brian Harris*

Left: Here are two views of the 3.30pm train from Kidderminster arriving at Bridgnorth on 27 April 2000, viewed from the footbridge linking the platforms. In the first, the locomotive dropping down the 1 in 100 gradient alongside Platform 1 is GWR 'Manor' Class 4-6-0 No 7802 *Bradley Manor*, at the head of seven BR standard coaches in 'carmine and cream' livery. The tracks on the right lead to the locomotive servicing facilities and Bridgnorth Locomotive Works. The excavated cutting side on the right is part of Panpudding Hill, an ancient fortification. *Geoff Sanders*

Right: No 7802 eases its train alongside the mellow stonework of Bridgnorth's main station building, completed for the formal opening of the Severn Valley line in 1862. Today it has listed historic building status, and is home to the ticket office, bar, sales shop and toilets. On Platform 2 the waiting shelter dates from the expansion of railway facilities here in 1887; until BR closed the line in 1963 this was the usual departure platform for trains continuing further northwards to Shrewsbury. *Geoff Sanders*

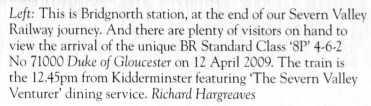

Left: This is Bridgnorth station, at the end of our Severn Valley Railway journey. And there are plenty of visitors on hand to view the arrival of the unique BR Standard Class '8P' 4-6-2 No 71000 *Duke of Gloucester* on 12 April 2009. The train is the 12.45pm from Kidderminster featuring 'The Severn Valley Venturer' dining service. *Richard Hargreaves*

Above left: From the station footbridge it is possible to view the range of locomotives in Bridgnorth yard. There is a distinctly South Wales 'feel' to the yard in this 31 July 2000 scene. GWR 0-6-0 saddle tank No 813 stands alongside the design that succeeded it at Duffryn Yard depot, Port Talbot, in the early 1930s, a GWR 0-6-0 pannier tank. This particular example, No 7714, was always based at Wolverhampton area depots, i.e. all

those coded '84' in BR days. It only reached South Wales in National Coal Board service in 1959, but the juxtaposition here is appropriate. The other SVR pannier, No 5764, equally inappropriately always a London area engine, is under repair on the right. *Rob Whale*

Above right: Turning slightly to the right from the previous view, on 25 June 1989, another member of the SVR home fleet, BR Standard Class '4MT' 4-6-0 No 75069, awaits the call to duty at Bridgnorth. This engine was built at Swindon in 1955, and served on all three divisions of the Southern Region of BR before withdrawal in 1966. After restoration from scrapyard condition, No 75069 proved very popular, both on the SVR and on main-line specials, between 1984 and 1994. *Steve Owen*

Above: Driver Frank Cronin awaits coaling at Kidderminster at 8.39 am on Saturday 24 March 2012 aboard Class '3F' 0-6-0 tank No 47406. *David Wilcock*

Right: Outside Bridgnorth Loco Works, Southern Region rebuilt 'West Country' 4-6-2 No 34027 *Taw Valley* looks ready for action in the summer of 1989. *Norman Kneale*

Opposite page left: On the adjacent track, or 'road' in British railway parlance, LMSR Stanier Class '8F' 2-8-0 No 48773 looks equally impressive during the evening of 13 January 2008. *John F. Stiles*

Above: At 7.23 am on Saturday 20 September 2008, Fireman Richard Silvester sets about watering loco No 813 at Kidderminster, in preparation for the journey ahead. *Kelly Moore*

Below: Fireman James Cooper and Driver Andy Christie are all set for a day on GWR 2-6-2 tank No 5164 at Kidderminster on 23 December 2011. *Bob Sweet*

The Severn Valley Railway
Gradient Profile

NOTES

This diagram shows in exaggerated form the gradients of the current Severn Valley Railway from Kidderminster to Bridgnorth.

Strictly, the section of line between Kidderminster and Bewdley Tunnel runs through the valley of the River Stour, and not the River Severn. (In fact it crosses the Stour by means of Falling Sands viaduct.) Shortly afterwards, Bewdley Tunnel pierces the ridge that separates the two rivers, and only beyond the tunnel is the line truly in the Severn valley.

On the diagram, the letter 'L' denotes level track. The numerals, for instance '112', denote a gradient of 1 in 112, which is either rising or falling according to the inclination of the top line. A gradient of 1 in 112 means that the line is rising or falling in the ratio of 1 foot vertically for every 112 feet horizontally.

The mileages shown at the foot of the diagram are recorded on mileposts every quarter of a mile along the track. From Kidderminster

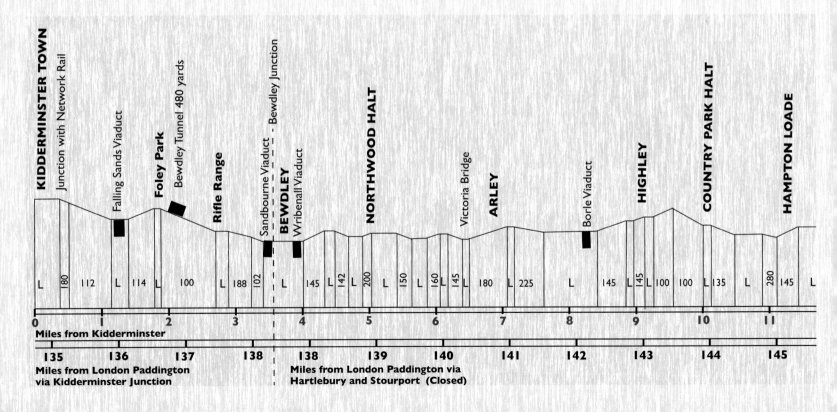

Junction to Bewdley Junction, the mileposts are on the west side of the line and record the mileages from London Paddington, via Didcot, Oxford, Worcester, Hartlebury and a reversal at Kidderminster Junction. This section of line comprises the whole length of the so-named 'Kidderminster Loop', constructed by the Great Western Railway in 1878. From Bewdley Junction northwards, the mileposts are generally on the east side of the line, and also record the mileages from London Paddington but via Didcot, Oxford, Worcester, Hartlebury and Stourport (thus measured via the now-closed original Severn Valley Railway route of 1862 from Hartlebury Junction to Bewdley Junction). The two different routes produce a 1 mile 9 chain reduction in milepost progression beyond Bewdley Junction, which is noticeable on the scale beneath the diagram. Note that, re the milepost in the photograph, the series of vertical 'strokes' beneath the mileage denotes the relevant number of quarter miles.

The other prominent and prolific posts on the side of the track are the gradient posts, positioned on the same side as the mileposts. They are located at places where there are significant changes in the gradient of the track. Semaphore arms that indicate and express the applicable gradients are attached to opposite sides of the main vertical post, as shown.

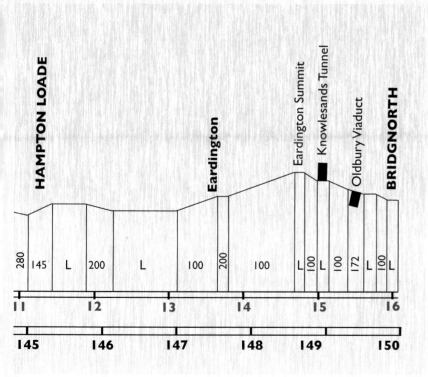

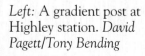

Above: A milepost, complete with owl. *David Pagett*

Left: A gradient post at Highley station. *David Pagett/Tony Bending*

GWR '5700' Class 0-6-0 pannier tank No 7714 provides a distinctive silhouette against the last dramatic rays of the sun at Rifle Range, making a spirited climb from Bewdley to the tunnel at the head of a Bridgnorth to Kidderminster train in January 1995. It is nearing the end of the day, and 7714's work is almost over...
Bob Green